CW01512472

Original title:
Amber Trails Inside the Fae Junk

Author: Sabrina Sarvik
ISBN HARDBACK: 978-1-80563-139-2
ISBN PAPERBACK: 978-1-80564-660-0

# A Dance with the Untold Dreams

In twilight's hush, the shadows play,
Whispers of wishes drift away.
A flicker of hope, a spark unseen,
In the heart of night, where dreams convene.

The moonlight weaves a silver thread,
Binding the stories long left unsaid.
With every heartbeat, secrets unfold,
Wrapped in the warmth of the night's cold hold.

Creatures of wonder, both wild and free,
Join the exuberant dance, a symphony.
Their laughter rings through the emerald glade,
In the embrace of magic, fears allayed.

From distant lands of the mind's own flight,
Echoes the call of the lost starlight.
Your spirit ascends, like smoke on the breeze,
In a realm where the mundane finds sweet release.

So waltz with the shadows, let whispers guide,
Embrace the unknown, with arms open wide.
For in this dance, where the untold gleams,
You'll find the truth hidden in your dreams.

### Whispers of the Gilded Path

Upon the golden leaves, they drift,
Soft murmurs of the past, a gift.
With every breath of autumn's grace,
A tale unfolds in this quiet place.

The winds weave through the branches high,
Secrets held beneath the sky.
Paths adorned with shades so bright,
Guide the wanderer lost in light.

Beneath the boughs, the stories play,
Of dreams bound tight in sweet array.
Each echo brushed by whispered sound,
In gilded glimmers, truths abound.

# Secrets in the Glittering Glade

In the glade where shadows dance,
Moonlit beams afford a chance.
Leaves like jewels under the night,
Hold the secrets of delight.

Fireflies flicker, soft and low,
Guiding hearts where few will go.
Each glimmer holds a tale untold,
Of bravery, of dreams so bold.

Ancient trees with bark so rough,
Guard the whispers, soft and tough.
In the silence, magic hums,
As nature's heart steadfastly drums.

## Echoes of Enchanted Wanderlust

Beneath the stars, the wanderers roam,
With hearts wide open, far from home.
Each step ignites the world anew,
In echoes of adventures true.

Misty mountains call the brave,
To chase the dreams they long to save.
With every breath, the journey starts,
As wanderlust ignites their hearts.

Across the valleys, secrets lie,
In whispers carried through the sky.
The pulse of earth, a siren's song,
In the dance of wild, where they belong.

## Luminous Footprints Beneath the Boughs

In moonlit paths where shadows bend,
Footprints light where dreams ascend.
Each step a brush with whispered fate,
Marking moments to celebrate.

Beneath the boughs of elder trees,
The air is thick with ancient ease.
Luminous trails of stardust shine,
Pointing to places where souls entwine.

As dawn unfolds, the past will gleam,
In every corner, in every dream.
Tread softly here, where legends meld,
In nature's arms, our hearts upheld.

# Dances with the Flickering Glimmers

In twilight's hush, where shadows play,
Glimmers dance, then fade away.
Whispers swirl beneath the trees,
Carried forth by gentle breeze.

Mirthful lights twirl, a lovely sight,
Step in rhythm, hearts take flight.
Every glow holds a hidden tale,
Of dreams and wishes that set sail.

Crickets chirp, a soft refrain,
Guiding souls to join the lane.
Moonlit paths invite the brave,
In this world, the lost can save.

Fingers brush against the night,
Ember sparks, a fleeting light.
Flickering hopes weave through the dark,
Each new step ignites a spark.

So dance we must, with joy unbound,
Among the glimmers, lost and found.
For in this magic, true hearts see,
The beauty in our reverie.

## The Lure of Forgotten Rabbit Holes

Nestled deep in the moonlit glade,
Secrets lie in shadows laid.
Rabbit holes twist, a pathway deep,
Where time stands still and dreams can leap.

In whispers soft, the echoes call,
A world where wonders never fall.
Curious hearts, brave and bold,
Venture forth into the old.

Forgotten tales of yesteryear,
Linger softly, crystal clear.
Each step leads to a hidden spring,
Where hopes arise and spirits sing.

Chasing whispers, soft and sweet,
In rabbit holes, our heartbeats greet.
Each twist and turn, a surprise anew,
Where fantasy greets reality too.

With a spark of magic in every glance,
We leap through the shadows, bold in our dance.
For within these tunnels, stories unfold,
A treasure trove of the brave and bold.

# Secrets Nestled Within Glimmering Ferns

Beneath the fern's emerald embrace,
Secrets hide in nature's space.
With swaying fronds, the whispers grow,
Of ancient tales we long to know.

In twilight's sheen, the shadows blend,
Stories linger, around the bend.
Glimmers twinkle, soft and bright,
Guiding wanderers through the night.

Every frond holds a dreamer's sigh,
In their dance, the wishes fly.
Cloaked in dew, the secrets gleam,
Enchanting souls to chase the dream.

Amongst the ferns, where time stands still,
Hearts discover a hidden thrill.
Nature's magic, a soft caress,
Invites us in, we feel its bless.

So linger here, in nature's hall,
Where secrets whisper, and shadows call.
In glimmering ferns, our dreams ignite,
Awakening wonders in the night.

## When Wishes Weave Through Moonbeams

In silver threads, the moonbeams glide,
Wishes dance, a soft tide.
Heartfelt hopes in the night sky,
Taking flight, we long to fly.

Beneath the stars, where dreams ignite,
Laughter echoes in the night.
Each twinkle sings of tales untold,
Of daring hearts and spirits bold.

Gentle whispers, secrets found,
In moonlit realms, our hopes abound.
Wishes weave through every beam,
Crafting magic, a waking dream.

With every flicker, we shall dare,
To chase the shadows, light as air.
For in this glow, our souls unfold,
In moonlit magic, our dreams are told.

So cast your wishes, let them soar,
For in the night, they search for more.
With moonbeams we'll create our way,
Lighting paths to a brighter day.

# Journeys in the Magical Maze

Through twisting paths where secrets dwell,
A whispering breeze casts a haunting spell.
Each turn unveils a page unturned,
With every choice, new wisdom earned.

Beneath the arch of tangled trees,
Imagination dances on a gentle breeze.
Lost and found in shadows deep,
Adventure calls, luring us to leap.

A glowing lantern in the night,
Chasing shadows, igniting flight.
With every step, the heart ignites,
In this maze of dreams and mystical sights.

Fabled creatures lurking near,
Their laughter ringing bright and clear.
In every twist, a tale unfolds,
Of courage rare and heroes bold.

So hand in hand, we'll wander far,
As tales unfold beneath the star.
Together we shall find our way,
In this magical maze of play.

# Fragments of Fantasy in the Forest

In forests deep, where whispers sing,
The echo of lost tales take wing.
Each leaf a story waiting to bloom,
Each shadow cast a sense of doom.

A brook babbles with secrets sweet,
While moonlit paths weave enchantments neat.
In every nook, a wonder hides,
With sparkling dreams the heart abides.

Fireflies dance like scattered stars,
Guiding wanderers from afar.
With every step, the magic swells,
Unlocking gates to ancient spells.

The breeze carries whispers of old,
Tales of bravery daring and bold.
In the embrace of the emerald ground,
Fragments of fantasy can be found.

So linger here and let time freeze,
In this enchanted realm of peace.
For in the forest's heart, we tread,
A world of dreams lies just ahead.

# Glimmers of Sprite-Lit Adventures

Amidst the glimmers of flickering lights,
Sprites flit and flutter through magical nights.
With laughter that's sweeter than morning dew,
They beckon us forth to join in the view.

Through valleys bright, in laughter we roam,
Where every sprig shows signs of home.
The whispers of joy and joy's sweet embrace,
Kindle our hearts in this timeless place.

With stardust trails leading the way,
The sprites weave enchantments that beckon to play.
In shimmering glades where dreams ignite,
We chase the horizon, guided by light.

Underneath the cloak of twilight's grace,
Adventure awaits, a breathless race.
With every heartbeat, we take flight,
In glimmers of sprite-lit adventures, our night.

So let the magic flow through our veins,
In a world where joy forever reigns.
With each winged friend, we'll soar, we'll sing,
In a tapestry woven of dreams we bring.

## Starlit Lanes of Enchantment

Along starlit lanes where dreams do tread,
Magic whispers to hearts that are led.
Each twinkle above a guiding grace,
In the stillness of night, we find our place.

With moonlight's kiss upon our skin,
We walk where adventures begin.
Every shadow a story yet told,
In starlit lanes, the night unfolds.

With every footstep, the cosmos sings,
Unlocking the wonder that starlight brings.
Beneath the celestial dome, we roam,
Finding enchantment in the night's foam.

The lanterns glimmer like lost wishes,
As we dance through a sea of hidden fishes.
Guided by the stars, spirits bright,
Starlit lanes cradle our delight.

So take my hand, let's wander far,
To realms of magic, where wonders are.
In the embrace of dreams, we will glide,
Through starlit lanes, side by side.

# Shimmering Dust on Wistful Wings

In twilight's hush, the shadows gleam,
On wings of whispers, gliding stream.
A sprinkle of dreams in vibrant dance,
Where moonbeams play, stars take a chance.

Each flicker tells of tales untold,
Of secrets wrapped in silver spun gold.
The nightingale sings to the starlit skies,
With shimmering dust, the past replies.

Through forests deep where fairies roam,
In every heart, they find a home.
Their laughter fills the air with grace,
In every soul, they leave a trace.

Beyond the mist where memories sleep,
In slumbering glades, the shadows creep.
With every sigh, enchantments weave,
A tapestry of what we believe.

So close your eyes, let longing soar,
On wistful wings, forevermore.
In shimmering dust, your dreams take flight,
And dance along the edge of night.

# Mysterious Roads of the Faery Realm

Along the paths where whispers call,
In moonlit meadows, shadows fall.
The faery roads twist and turn,
In every corner, secrets burn.

With petals soft beneath your feet,
Each step reveals a mystic beat.
The air alive with laughter's ring,
As night unveils her hidden spring.

In glades where time slips through the seams,
And stars ignite our wildest dreams.
The echoes of an ageless song,
Guide weary hearts where they belong.

Beneath the boughs of ancient trees,
The fae converse upon the breeze.
With glances veiled in twilight's grace,
They guard the magic of this place.

So wander forth on paths unknown,
Through realms where fantasy has grown.
In every turn, let wonder dwell,
Mysterious roads, a faery spell.

# Rustling Leaves of Ethereal Lores

In canopies where soft winds sigh,
Rustling leaves with stories nigh.
They murmur of the past, untold,
In whispers wrapped in hues of gold.

Each leaf a page, each branch a line,
Of tales that fade, yet still align.
The forest glows with memories bright,
Illuminating the heart of night.

In shadows cast by twilight's grace,
The faery folk in dance embrace.
Their laughter beckons like a dream,
As moonlight weaves an argent seam.

A symphony of life unfolds,
In rustling leaves, the night beholds.
With every breath, a magic stirs,
In nature's heart, where wonder purrs.

So tarry not where time flows free,
For in each rustle, there lies a key.
To ethereal lores, old as the trees,
In their embrace, find joy and peace.

# Lost Treasures in the Enchanted Grove

In woods where twilight softly glows,
And secrets whispered, gently flows.
Lost treasures hide in every glade,
In tales of old, their worth conveyed.

With every step, adventure waits,
As faery doors reveal their fates.
The gleam of treasures, faint and bright,
Awakens dreams that take to flight.

Amongst the roots and tangled vines,
In hidden nooks, the magic shines.
A crystal brook sings songs of yore,
Inviting hearts to seek and soar.

In laughter shared and stories spun,
The treasures found when day is done.
An emerald glow, a sapphire's gleam,
In every heart, a glimmering dream.

So venture forth, let courage rise,
In enchanted groves beneath the skies.
For every lost treasure found anew,
A promise made in whispers true.

# The Enchantment of Hidden Trails

In the woods where whispers dwell,
Ancient secrets cast their spell.
Footsteps follow winding ways,
Where sunlight dances, shadows play.

Leaves above in hues of gold,
Stories of the brave and bold.
Every bend a tale unfolds,
Of dreams and wishes softly told.

Amidst the ferns, the silence speaks,
In hidden nooks, the magic peaks.
For those who seek with open hearts,
A world of wonders gently starts.

A glimmering path, a distant call,
The forest beckons, enthralling all.
With every step, enchantment grows,
In nature's realm, where beauty flows.

Hands of shadows, fingers of light,
Guide the traveler through the night.
With every sigh, the journey swells,
In hidden trails, the heart compels.

## Faery Glimmers in the Dappled Light

In the glen where faeries play,
Dappled light marks the way.
Gossamer wings and laughter bright,
Weave the magic of the night.

Twinkling stars in twilight's embrace,
Softly glowing, a sacred space.
Whispers of the winds declare,
That wondrous beings linger there.

Petals bloom with joy divine,
Each one hosts a little sign.
In every shadow, joy abounds,
Where love and laughter dance around.

A symphony of nature's tune,
Crickets chirrup, under the moon.
With each flicker and every beam,
Reality bends, blurs into dream.

Glimpers spark like fireflies,
Mapping paths where magic lies.
Underneath the leafy dome,
Faery glimmers guide us home.

## Spirit Wind Beneath the Wistful Canopy

Underneath the ancient trees,
The spirit wind hums with ease.
Carrying tales from times of old,
In whispers faint and secrets bold.

With every rustle of the leaves,
A story spins, the heart believes.
Echoes dance on gentle sighs,
As if the forest softly cries.

Branches sway and shadows bend,
To whom do these soft murmurs send?
A call to those who seek the truth,
In hidden corners lies pure youth.

The tapestry of life entwined,
Each breeze a prayer, each breath aligned.
Wistful canopy stretches wide,
Embracing dreams that never hide.

With open hearts and trusting minds,
We follow where the spirit finds.
To wander lost in nature's thrall,
Where all are one, and none are small.

## Mystical Paths Through the Verdant Realm

Woven trails through emerald bliss,
Laden with the morning mist.
Each step upon the soft, cool earth,
A promise of the journey's worth.

Meandering streams, a silver thread,
Guide seekers where fears are shed.
With open arms, the green woods sway,
Inviting souls to dance and play.

The call of birds in jubilant flight,
Fills the heart with pure delight.
In every corner, colors bright,
Reveal the magic held in light.

Mossy rocks and wildflower blooms,
Softly cradle nature's tunes.
An orchestra of rustling leaves,
And buzzing bees that weave and cleave.

As twilight falls, the realm transforms,
With shadows casting hidden forms.
Mystical paths through time and space,
In every heartbeat, we find our place.

# Secrets from Beneath the Celestial Canopy

In shadows deep where starlights weep,
The whispers stir, where dreams do creep.
Among the roots of ancient trees,
The night unveils its mysteries.

A silver mist, a hidden path,
Where moonlight bathes in gentle bath.
Each secret holds a tale untold,
Of magic, power, myths of old.

Through branches twist, the night winds sing,
A lullaby of hidden things.
With every breath, the night unfolds,
As time reveals its precious holds.

Ethereal glows on dewdrop blades,
In silence held, where dusk cascades.
Each darting glance, a fleeting chance,
To grasp a moment's fleeting dance.

So linger where the shadows play,
And listen close; their secrets sway.
For beneath the celestial dome,
The ancient roots are calling home.

# Glistening Reflections of the Wild

In forest glades where wild things roam,
The sunlight sings to every loam.
With colors bright, the day ignites,
A canvas spun of nature's sights.

Each meadow breathes, a vibrant hue,
Where petals soft in morning dew.
The breeze, it dances, sweet and light,
In harmony with day and night.

The rivers laugh, their waters clear,
In crystal paths, their joy sincere.
They mirror skies, a shifting show,
Of fleeting clouds and sunlit glow.

With every step on leaf-strewn ground,
The magic's felt, in silence found.
The whispers rise, as shadows blend,
In nature's arms, where dreams ascend.

So wander deep, where wild things play,
And feel the pulse of earth's ballet.
For in each glance, a story lies,
In glistening reflections, nature sighs.

# Whispers of the Silvery Spray

Upon the cliffs where waters crash,
The rivers weave in endless flash.
With every drop, a story spins,
Of journeys lost and places wins.

The ocean's heart, a gate to dreams,
In rippling waves, the starlight gleams.
With every wave, a secret told,
Of treasures deep and legends bold.

The mist that hugs the morning shore,
Invites the wanderer to explore.
With salty air and sunlit grace,
The world feels wide, a vast embrace.

Each surge of tide, a timeless dance,
In silver spray, lost souls advance.
Their whispers carried on the breeze,
In symphonies of ancient seas.

So let the currents guide your way,
To realms where time and dreams can play.
For in each splash, the magic sways,
In whispers soft of the silvery spray.

## Wayward Spirits Among the Leaves

In gentle rustle, soft and low,
The spirits call from earth below.
Among the leaves, they weave their tales,
In whispered breaths as daylight pales.

Through tangled roots and mossy beds,
Where footsteps fade and silence spreads,
They dance like shadows, light and free,
Entwined with every friendly tree.

Their laughter rings in twilight's hues,
In magic spun from midnight's muse.
With echoes faint, their warmth draws near,
As mysteries loom, so crystal clear.

The silver moon, a watchful eye,
Beneath its glow, the world awry.
For wayward spirits seek to blend,
In nature's heart, where pathways end.

So tread the paths where whispers guide,
And let the winds of fate abide.
For in the woods, the spirits dwell,
In tales of old, where dreams compel.

## Whispers of Gossamer Dust

In twilight's glow, soft voices sing,
Of dreams untold, on gossamer wing.
The stars above whisper secrets near,
As night unfolds, we draw them near.

With every breeze, a tale unfurls,
Of ancient woods and hidden pearls.
The shadows dance, a waltz so light,
In silver beams of soft moonlight.

A flicker here, a glimmer there,
The night conceals with artful flair.
Through leaves that shiver in the dark,
Awakens hope, igniting spark.

The air is thick with promises sweet,
Where dreams and reality gently meet.
In whispers soft as morning dew,
The magic lives, forever true.

## Secrets Beneath the Glittering Canopy

Under the boughs, where shadows creep,
The secrets rest, in silence they sleep.
Each leaf a tale, each branch a verse,
In shimmering light, the worlds disperse.

Whispers of ages, caressed by time,
In hidden paths, the echoes chime.
The wind weaves stories, old and wise,
Beneath the stars, where dreams arise.

A hidden realm, adorned in night,
With every step, we draw delight.
In moonlit glades, the magic glows,
In every heart, the wonder grows.

Beneath the canopy, hope takes flight,
In tangled roots, our spirits ignite.
The secrets linger, waiting to share,
In whispers tender, soft as air.

## Echoes from the Enchanted Thicket

In thickets deep, where shadows play,
The echoes dance, and dreams sway.
A rustling sound, a fleeting sigh,
In every corner, magic lies.

The moonlit path, a silver thread,
Guides wandering souls where few have tread.
Through tangled vines, and whispering trees,
The heart can feel the gentle breeze.

Hidden echoes, stories vast,
Of ancient times, forever cast.
In every knot, in every scar,
Tales of the brave, and those who've far.

The thicket hums with life anew,
As twilight skies shift from gray to blue.
In enchanted realms, we lose our way,
Finding treasures in the day.

## Worn Relics of the Hidden Realm

Amidst the ruins, history weaves,
Worn relics whisper, tales of thieves.
Each cracked stone a portrait drawn,
In echoes past, where dreams were born.

The air is thick with stories old,
Of bravery bold and hearts of gold.
In every shadow, secrets blend,
A time forgotten, where legends mend.

The relics sigh with stories lost,
Of love and war, and the price of cost.
With every breath, the whispers cling,
To every heart, the memories sing.

In the hidden realm, we wander free,
Among the remnants of what used to be.
The heart remembers, the soul will find,
The echoes linger, forever entwined.

## Colors of the Unfathomable Glade

In the heart where shadows dream,
A tapestry of colors gleam.
Mossy greens and emerald lies,
Beneath the watchful, azure skies.

Whispers dance on twilight air,
Golden rays weave through the lair.
Crimson blooms in bursts of flair,
Secrets hidden everywhere.

Winding paths of ochre gold,
Stories ripe for hearts to hold.
Silken petals touch the breeze,
A melody that charms the trees.

Deep within the veiled embrace,
Nature's wonders find their place.
Dappled light through branches flows,
In the glade where magic grows.

Every hue a tale to tell,
In this world where dreams compel.
Colors vivid, spirits free,
In the glade, a symphony.

# Enchanted Echoes Through the Night

Beneath the shroud of midnight's cloak,
The moon's soft laughter gently spoke.
Stars like lanterns twinkled bright,
Guiding wanderers into night.

Whispers carried on the breeze,
Ancient tales beneath the trees.
Shadows dance in silver's glow,
Where secrets of the dark unfold.

Echoes weave like silky threads,
Through the dreams of sleepy heads.
A night's embrace, both sweet and sly,
Opens windows to the sky.

In this realm of mystic flight,
All is possible, pure delight.
Each echoed laugh, each sigh once known,
Is a reminder, we're not alone.

Through the gloaming, hearts take wing,
Magic hums, and nightbirds sing.
In every note, a promise swells,
An enchanted night with endless spells.

## Pilgrimage of the Lost Glow

They journey forth through mist and dark,
Upon a road where dreams embark.
With lanterns held high, hopes ignite,
In search of warmth on this chill night.

Footsteps soft on cobbled stone,
They wander where the wild winds moan.
The past entwined in whispered song,
They seek the glow that feels so wrong.

Beneath the shroud of ancient oaks,
The wanderers share their tender yokes.
Each heartbeat blends with nature's sighs,
A pilgrimage beneath the skies.

Yearning hearts in the cool night air,
Together they weave their silent prayer.
For light anew, for love to grow,
To find the path where lost hearts glow.

With every step, the shadows fade,
As memories dance in twilight's parade.
Their spirits lifted, hopes bestowed,
On this lost glow, they found their road.

# The Tangle of Whimsical Groves

In the woods where wonders play,
A tangle of dreams, night and day.
Branches twist in a playful gleam,
Where fairies weave the threads of dream.

Mushrooms sprout in hues so bright,
Glimmers of magic invite delight.
Each pathway spun with laughter's thread,
In the grove where fantasies spread.

Tiny creatures find their homes,
Under leaves, the mischief roams.
A world alive with stories told,
In the silent language of the bold.

Wayward paths that tease and twine,
A splendorous dance, a secret sign.
In every nook, a tale unfolds,
Of daring hearts and dreams retold.

Let your spirit loose and free,
In these groves of whimsy, be.
For here in this enchanted place,
Every corner holds a trace.

# The Glimmering Veil of Wild Fancies

In the hush of twilight's grace,
Dreams take flight in silver space.
Whispers dance on dewy leaves,
Crafting tales that heart believes.

Softly glowing, wishes weave,
A tapestry of what we receive.
Wondrous sights, like starlit streams,
Inviting us to chase our dreams.

Hidden realms where shadows play,
Frolic in the moonbeam's sway.
Mirages bloom in secret night,
Filling hearts with sweet delight.

Glimmers beckon, secrets call,
In the magical, we lose it all.
The veil, a dance of hopes untold,
Envelops us in stories bold.

Beyond horizons, truth can hide,
In every heartbeat, magic bides.
Forever drawn to fancies wild,
In every dream, we're free and wild.

# Twinkling Stars on a Misty Trail

A path adorned with dreams so bright,
Twinkling stars, they steal the night.
Misty whispers, soft as dew,
Guide us where the wonders brew.

Footprints lead through fragrant trees,
Carried on a gentle breeze.
Secrets twirl in moonlit beams,
Stirring echoes of our themes.

Delicate charms of nature's art,
Draw us close, ignite the heart.
Each step reveals a hidden gleam,
Igniting sparks of every dream.

Through tangled vines and thickets wide,
Adventure waits, our hearts the guide.
Oh, how the night begins to sway,
As dreams awaken on the way.

With every star, a wish we make,
Leaving trails of hope awake.
A symphony of night prevails,
Upon this path, our spirit sails.

## Enchanted Whispers in the Night

Veils of silence cloak the air,
Magic lingers everywhere.
Enchanted whispers softly flow,
Wrapped in twilight's gentle glow.

Ancient trees, with stories vast,
Hold the echoes of the past.
Every sigh, a breath of lore,
In the night, we seek for more.

Stars align in secret song,
Guiding hearts where we belong.
Voices call from shadows deep,
In their arms, we drift to sleep.

Moonbeams dance on misty streams,
Carrying our wildest dreams.
Sparks of wonder fill the sky,
With every breath, we learn to fly.

Hold the magic, clasp it tight,
In the woven threads of night.
Awake, arise to realms so bright,
As enchanted whispers take their flight.

# Moonlit Paths of Charmed Discoveries

Beneath the glow of silver light,
Lies a path, both strange and bright.
Mysteries whisper in the air,
Charmed discoveries linger there.

Along the trails where shadows roam,
Nature sings of distant home.
Every glance unveils a tale,
In moonlit mist, our dreams set sail.

Glowing orbs of dreams take flight,
Sketching wonders in the night.
Twinkling realms of magic spin,
Inviting us to look within.

Trails of starlight beckon near,
Guiding us through loss and cheer.
Each discovery a brand new spark,
Illuminated in the dark.

Hold these visions, pure and bright,
As we wander through the night.
Moonlit paths, forever free,
Charmed discoveries, just you and me.

# Secrets of the Woodland Fairies

In the hush of the moonlit glade,
Whispers dance on the evening air,
Elfin laughter, a sweet serenade,
Secrets held, hidden with care.

Beneath the boughs, where shadows play,
Glimmers of magic weave through the night,
Gentle wings brush the golden hay,
Stars flicker soft, lending their light.

Grasses sway with a knowing sigh,
Mysteries twine in the tangled leaves,
Silent wonders, oh how they fly,
In a world where belief retrieves.

From dappled woods, they flit and gleam,
Spinning tales of both joy and woe,
Each tale a thread in a grander dream,
A tapestry woven with love's gentle glow.

Listen close, for the fairies sing,
Songs of old, of hope and delight,
In every heart, they leave a spring,
A quiet glow in the deep of night.

## Flickering Embers in the Fabled Wild

In the heart of the forest, embers glow,
Fables whisper tales of courage bright,
Guiding wanderers where wild winds blow,
Through the shadows of the gathering night.

Beasts of lore roam the ancient paths,
Every rustle speaks of wondrous things,
Secrets woven in nature's swaths,
Flickering dreams on ethereal wings.

Stars are born from the flames of lore,
Dancing softly on the velvet sky,
Echoes vibrate from the forest floor,
As legends awaken and softly sigh.

In the flicker of dusk, a tale unfolds,
Of knights and maidens, and daring quests,
A journey sought in the silence bold,
Where hope and wonder wear silver vests.

Follow the gleam through the sylvan deep,
The embers lead where the brave can tread,
For in their glow, even dreams shall leap,
And weave new stories where none have led.

## The Forgotten Way of Elfin Secrets

In a glen where the moonlight falls,
Elfin secrets softly twine,
Lost in time, where magic calls,
A path forgotten, yet divine.

Whispers drift on the morning breeze,
Carrying tales of long ago,
In the rustling leaves, the heart agrees,
Every secret a chance to grow.

Footsteps trace where the ancients tread,
In circles drawn by time's slow hands,
A world awakened from dreams long dead,
Revealing truth in forgotten lands.

Underneath the arching trees,
Shadows dance with a fleeting grace,
Elfin laughter rides with ease,
In the hidden corners of this place.

Journey forth with an open heart,
Find the path where the starlight weaves,
Embrace the magic, take your part,
In the lore that the forest leaves.

# Lanterns of the Mischievous Wood

In the wood where the lanterns gleam,
Mischief sparkles in the hazy air,
A twinkling laughter, a waking dream,
Frolicsome sprites dance without a care.

Through the fog, where the moonbeams play,
Shadows stretch and twist with glee,
Chasing secrets that flit away,
Elusive as the softest breeze.

Twinkling lights guide the lost at night,
With every flicker, a path revealed,
Radiant joys in the soft twilight,
Mischiefs shared, their hearts unsealed.

Each lantern holds a tale untold,
Of playful pranks and fleeting chance,
In the depths of the wood, both brave and bold,
Whispers echo in a playful dance.

So venture forth with a curious mind,
In the mischievous wood of ancient lore,
Where magic thrives, and charms unwind,
And every turn holds adventures galore.

# The Magic of Tattered Pages

In dusty corners, secrets dwell,
Where tattered pages weave their spell.
With whispered ink and faded lines,
A world awakens where magic twines.

Each flip reveals a story old,
In worn-out tales, vast dreams unfold.
Characters dance on fragile sheets,
In every word, the heart still beats.

The scent of parchment, sweet and warm,
Beneath the moon, ideas swarm.
Imagination's vivid flight,
Guides us through the starry night.

With every crease, a path is found,
In ancient tomes, our souls unbound.
A spark ignites, the journey starts,
In tattered pages, magic imparts.

So turn the leaves, embrace the lore,
For in those words, we long for more.
In twilight's hue, as shadows play,
We find our dreams in tattered fray.

# Celestial Petals in the Twilight

Upon the breeze, a soft embrace,
Celestial petals dance with grace.
In twilight's glow, a gentle sigh,
They weave a tale against the sky.

Each blossom holds a wish so bright,
Whispers of secrets in the night.
As stars emerge and shimmer low,
The petals tell of love's sweet flow.

Moonlight filters through the trees,
Guiding dreams on fragrant breeze.
With every step, our spirits rise,
As magic blooms beneath the skies.

In dusky hues, the silence sings,
Awakening hope, on gentle wings.
The twilight bathes our hearts in gold,
As endless stories unfold, untold.

So let us walk where shadows fall,
Amongst the petals, heed their call.
In every soft and tender sway,
The celestial dance will lead the way.

## Wistful Glimmers in Moonlit Groves

In moonlit groves where shadows play,
Wistful glimmers guide the way.
With every rustle, dreams take flight,
In the quiet of the starlit night.

The trees are whispers, soft and clear,
Echoing tales of those we hold dear.
As silver beams touch ancient bark,
Memories linger, igniting spark.

A gentle hush binds earth and sky,
As mystical creatures flit on by.
In every glimmer, magic weaves,
A tapestry of hopes and thieves.

The nightingale in songful trance,
Lures weary souls to join the dance.
With every note, the heart beats bold,
In moonlit groves, the stories unfold.

So quiet your mind, and take a breath,
Embrace the magic found in death.
For in the darkness, light shall grow,
In wistful glimmers of moonlit groves.

# Threads of Silken Starlight

In twilight's weave, a tale is spun,
Threads of starlight, softly run.
A shimmering path where dreams collide,
In cosmic realms, our hearts abide.

Each thread is woven with a wish,
In silken strands, a starry swish.
With every pull, the heavens sigh,
As whispers dance in the endless sky.

As dawn approaches, colors blend,
A tapestry that has no end.
In every glow, our spirits soar,
With threads of starlight, we explore.

Let hope be anchored in the night,
With each entwined, a radiant light.
For in this cosmic, endless frame,
Each silken thread, a spark of flame.

So dream anew with every breath,
In starlight's arms, surrender death.
As wonder weaves through night's expanse,
We find our place in this grand dance.

## The Faery's Hidden Nook

In shadows soft where whispers sing,
The faery dances, light on wing.
Beneath the boughs, in twilight's gleam,
They weave a world, a secret dream.

With petals bright and dew so clear,
They guard the heart of forests near.
In laughter's hush, they spin their spells,
Where magic stirs and silence dwells.

At dusk they twirl, a gilded glow,
Their laughter rings like winds that blow.
A hidden nook, where none may tread,
A universe, where joy is spread.

Through leafy paths and moonlit streams,
They chase the echoes of pure dreams.
Their realm awaits, with stars in tune,
In faery lights beneath the moon.

So close your eyes and breathe the air,
Feel magic whisper in your hair.
For in the nook where faeries play,
Is where your heart will long to stay.

# Shards of Ancient Laughter

In crumbling halls where shadows creep,
Resonates a laughter, rich and deep.
Each echo holds a tale long told,
Of ages past and dreams of old.

The crickets chirp in rhythms sweet,
While dust motes dance on nimble feet.
With every gust, the windows sigh,
As whispers weave through the night sky.

Secrets hide in every stone,
In laughter shared, we are not alone.
The past and present gently blend,
In shards of joy that never end.

With open hearts, we roam the past,
Where ancient laughter still holds fast.
In twilight hours, we see it clear,
The magic lives, forever near.

So treasure the moments, let them soar,
For laughter's light will guide us more.
In every smile, in every gleam,
Lie shards of joy, like hidden dreams.

# Dreamscapes in Celestial Hues

In realms where starlight paints the night,
Dreamscapes bloom, a wondrous sight.
With colors bright, like whispers sweet,
They beckon souls on nimble feet.

Beneath the arc of cosmic gleam,
We sail on tides of thought and dream.
Each canvas swirls with hopes anew,
Awakening the heart's true hue.

The moonlight glistens, softly falls,
In depths of night, a voice that calls.
Through veils of mist, the dreams pursue,
In vibrant shades of silver blue.

With every breath, the colors shift,
As dreams and starlight intertwine in gift.
In celestial hues, we rise and glide,
On wings of wonder, let us ride.

So close your eyes, embrace the flight,
For in these dreams, we claim our light.
From dawn till dusk, our spirits soar,
In dreamscapes rich, forevermore.

# A Collection of Unseen Journeys

Upon the path where few have trod,
A world unfolds, a quiet nod.
Through fields of mystery, we roam,
Each step we take, we find our home.

The whispers call from ancient trees,
Telling tales upon the breeze.
In every shadow, stories lie,
A collection of journeys, soaring high.

With footprints left on winding trails,
We carve our dreams with hope-filled sails.
In every glance, a memory blooms,
In unseen journeys, magic looms.

So take a breath, and feel the air,
For every journey holds a prayer.
In every heart, a story yearns,
In unseen paths, the world still turns.

Let courage guide you, step with grace,
For every journey finds its place.
In moments shared, we weave our art,
A collection of journeys, heart to heart.

# Mysteries Cradled in Twilight's Embrace

In shadows deep where whispers weave,
The stars alight, our souls believe.
A crescent moon, a silver gleam,
Beneath its glow, we softly dream.

The night unveils a world untold,
With secrets hidden, waiting bold.
A dance of fireflies, soft and bright,
In twilight's arms, they take their flight.

The ancient trees, with branches wide,
Guard paths where dreams and wishes bide.
Each rustling leaf tells tales of yore,
As shadows play on forest floor.

An echo calls from realms unseen,
Through tangled roots where hopes convene.
In the twilight's tender clasp,
The night's embrace becomes our grasp.

Here in the dusk, our hearts align,
As magic stirs through space and time.
With every breath, the secrets gleam,
In twilight's arms, we weave our dream.

## Fragments of Ethereal Whimsy

A gentle laugh, a flicker bright,
In dreams that dance upon the light.
With pixie dust and whispers sweet,
The world unveils, a playful treat.

The clouds take shapes, a fleeting guise,
As time flows softly, drifting skies.
With every twirl, the moments gleam,
In vivid hues like painted dream.

In frolic fields where faeries play,
The sunbeams weave a golden ray.
Among the blooms, a tale is spun,
Of laughter shared by everyone.

A secret nook 'neath willow's sway,
Where stories hum and music play.
With melodies of soft delight,
Each note a spark, a twinkling light.

In fragments bright, we find our way,
As whimsy takes the lead today.
A tapestry of joys so clear,
In every smile, we hold it dear.

## Secrets Spun from Woodland Memories

In twilight's hush, the secrets weave,
Through twisted roots, the past believes.
A gentle breeze, a sighing sound,
In every nook, lost dreams abound.

The laughter of a brook nearby,
Reflects the joy of days gone by.
Amidst the ferns and ancient moss,
Each fragrant breeze, a gentle toss.

The echoing calls of nightingale,
Spin stories soft, like whispered tales.
Beneath the boughs, where shadows merge,
Memories rise, a fleeting surge.

With every footfall, time does wane,
In woodland paths, we feel the reign.
Of moments cast in twilight's glow,
In earthy beds where secrets flow.

Through emerald glades, we drift and roam,
In magical realms, we find our home.
As twilight wraps in velvet nights,
We gather dreams like shining lights.

# Glinting Wonders of the Dusty Path

Along the way, where wildflowers bloom,
The dusty path begins to loom.
With every step, a tale is spun,
As golden rays embrace the sun.

The pebbles glint like stars aglow,
In whispers soft, as breezes flow.
A journey taken, hearts in tow,
With every turn, new wonders grow.

The trees lean in with secrets shared,
In knots of bark, the stories dared.
With every leaf that flutters down,
A treasure found, a whispered crown.

Each season paints in hues so bright,
As time unfolds through day and night.
The dusty trail, a winding song,
Where every soul begins to belong.

With glimmering dreams and hopes to find,
The wonders call, both fierce and kind.
As we embrace the path ahead,
In every step, our hearts are fed.

# Sylvan Dreams Between the Shadows

In whispers soft, the willows sway,
Beneath the boughs where fairies play.
Moonbeams dance on leaves of jade,
In twilight dreams, our hopes are laid.

A silver brook sings sweet and clear,
It carries tales for those who hear.
The ancient pines, they stand so tall,
Guarding secrets of the forest's call.

Through tangled roots, the magic flows,
In hidden nooks, enchantment grows.
A symphony of night and song,
Where we, the dreamers, all belong.

The shadows weave a tapestry,
Of long-lost lore and mystery.
Each rustle speaks of times gone by,
In sylvan dreams beneath the sky.

With every breath, the essence blends,
Of nature's magic that transcends.
And in the dark, our spirits soar,
Forever bound to ancient lore.

# Fragments of Forgotten Magic

Scattered shards of yesteryear,
In dusty tomes, the spells appear.
In whispered lines, they softly call,
Remnants of power, cherished by all.

Through crumbling pages, echoes sigh,
Of sorcerers who aimed for the sky.
Each fragment glows, a beacon bright,
In shadows deep, igniting light.

Beneath the starlit canopy,
They weave their fates in harmony.
With every breath, the magic swells,
In ancient woods where wonder dwells.

The line between the real and dream,
Is stitched with threads of silver seam.
In every word, a spell reborn,
Crafting worlds from tales forlorn.

So gather 'round, ye seekers bold,
The wonders of the past unfold.
In fragments lost, our hearts shall find,
The magic whispers through the mind.

# Nectar of the Twilight Forest

In twilight's glow, the blossoms gleam,
Their fragrance lingers, light as dream.
A nectar sweet from petals drawn,
Awakens magic with the dawn.

The fireflies twinkle, like drifting stars,
In the hush of night, they chase our scars.
With every sip from nature's cup,
We find our strength, we lift right up.

The brook babbles secrets in the dark,
A soft serenade, a tender spark.
Through bramble paths and emerald glade,
We wander forth, in dreams arrayed.

Each shadow holds a story long,
A symphony of the earth's sweet song.
In twilight's thrall, we seek and roam,
Finding solace, finding home.

With every step, enchantment weaves,
Through whispering woods, where magic cleaves.
In twilight's hush, we are reborn,
Drinking deeply from the morn.

# Flickering Lights of the Wandering Realm

Upon the crest of evening's breath,
Flickering lights defy the death.
They pulse and dance, with wild delight,
In the wandering realm of shadows' flight.

Each glow a wish, each spark a dream,
In the tapestry of the moonlight's beam.
With every flicker, a journey awaits,
Through hidden paths and mystic gates.

The air hums soft with ancient tunes,
As starry spirits grace the dunes.
They guide the heart, they soothe the soul,
In wandering realms, we are made whole.

From whispered winds to sighing trees,
A symphony of memories flows with ease.
Through twilight's grasp, our hearts ignite,
Chasing the dawn, embracing night.

In flickering hues, the stories blend,
Of worlds forgotten, where dreamers mend.
As stars fall down, we take our flight,
In the wandering realm of purest light.

# Luminescence in the Wildwood

In the heart of the wood, a glow,
Gentle lights dance, weaving slow.
Whispers of magic, soft and bright,
Guide us deeper into the night.

Beneath ancient boughs, secrets dwell,
Each petal a tale, each stone a spell.
Stars intertwined with the earth below,
In radiant hues, their stories flow.

From twilight's veil, a soft refrain,
Breath of the wild, a silvery train.
With every step, the shadows sigh,
In the wildwood, where spirits fly.

A flicker of hope in whispered leaves,
The heartache of time, the joy it weaves.
In the twilight, we stand, aware,
Of the luminescent magic we share.

So come, dear wanderer, lift your gaze,
In this enchanted wood, lose the maze.
For in the gleam where the wild things play,
You'll find a spark that won't drift away.

## Beneath Mossy Canopies of Wonder

Beneath the green where shadows cling,
Mossy blankets cradle spring.
With every breath, the forest hums,
In sync with the rhythm of drumming drums.

Ferns unfurl like secrets kept,
In the stillness, dreams are swept.
Each twilight whispers, a gentle kiss,
Promising wonders that none would miss.

Through tangled roots and shimmering dew,
Life dances lightly, all fresh and new.
An echo of laughter, a hint of grace,
In the stillness, we find our place.

Above us sprawls a treetop choir,
Singing stories that never tire.
In the cool embrace of mossy shade,
Together, our fears begin to fade.

So venture forth with heart unbound,
Where the wild and wondrous abound.
In this realm where dreams ascend,
Beneath the canopies, find a friend.

## Trinkets of Forgotten Dreams

In the glade where wishes lay,
Trinkets of dreams from yesterday.
Scattered treasures, glimmers bright,
Whispering tales of lost delight.

A locket, a ribbon, a dusty book,
Each holds magic, if one but took.
With every glance, a story stirs,
In this haven where memory blurs.

Softly, the breeze carries a song,
Of laughter and joy that once belonged.
Yet in shadows where silence creeps,
The essence of wonder forever keeps.

Upon the winds of time's embrace,
These trinkets shimmer, a whispered trace.
In the arms of the night, let's take our flight,
And reclaim those dreams, lost from sight.

For in the echoes of what has been,
Lie fragments of hope, to begin again.
Gather these treasures, each delicate seam,
And weave once more the fabric of dream.

# A Dance Among Twinkling Shadows

In twilight's glow, the shadows sway,
A dance of phantoms, both wild and fey.
With flickering lights, they swirl and twine,
Binding their secrets in rhythms divine.

Moonlight spills like silver lace,
Kissing the earth with a soft embrace.
The night unfolds in a waltz surreal,
As magic lingers, an unbroken seal.

Through the woodland paths we roam,
With each footfall, we find our home.
In the symphony of night's gentle sigh,
We join in the dance, you and I.

Beneath the stars, the shadows weave,
Stories of old, dreams to believe.
In the pulse of night, our spirits rise,
A tapestry spun from starlit skies.

So heed the call of the twinkling night,
Embrace the shadows, hold them tight.
For in this dance among whispers sweet,
We find our heart's enchanting beat.

## Echoes of the Sylph's Secrets

In whispers laced with dew and sighs,
The sylphs dance 'neath moonlit skies.
They weave their tales with gentle grace,
In hidden glades, in twilight's embrace.

With each flutter, magic stirs,
A melody that softly purrs.
In glimmers bright, their laughter flows,
Ethereal dreams the forest knows.

In shadows deep where secrets play,
They guard the night, then slip away.
A tender touch upon the breeze,
A glimpse of wonder in the trees.

Oh, listen close, the leaves will tell,
Of ancient charms, where spirits dwell.
In every gust, their echoes blend,
A spell of light that will not end.

## Celestial Dust on Nature's Canvas

Among the leaves, a tapestry,
Of stardust bright for all to see.
With golden threads and midnight hues,
Nature's brush, a palette bruised.

Each bloom and bud, a story spun,
Under the gaze of a beckoning sun.
In violet skies, the hues will dance,
A cosmic swirl, a fleeting chance.

The flowers whisper secrets sweet,
Of worlds unseen, where dreams compete.
A painter's hand on morning's dew,
Sketches a dawn of hope anew.

Among the trees, the colors blend,
A symphony as daylight bends.
In every shade, a wish is cast,
Celestial dust, a spell that lasts.

# Fantasies Found Among the Fabled Roots

Beneath the earth where legends sleep,
The fabled roots in silence creep.
In whispered tales of ancient lore,
A world awakens, rich in core.

With every twist, a secret shared,
In tangled dreams, the lost repaired.
A glimpse of history, time untold,
Where fairies play and magic's bold.

In shadowed depths, the spirits dance,
In playful jest and daring chance.
Each root a journey, a path to find,
Where heart and whimsy intertwine.

Through whispers low, they beckon near,
To valleys deep, devoid of fear.
In twilight's hush where phantoms roam,
We find our truths in silence comb.

So seek the wonders, delve and dive,
Among the roots, the dreams arrive.
In fables, lost and found anew,
The heart of magic beats for you.

## Glistening Realms of Twilight Dreams

As twilight drapes the world in gold,
A secret realm begins to unfold.
With glistening lights that dance afar,
A hush of night, the evening star.

The shadows stretch, a velvet hand,
Inviting dreams to take their stand.
In every corner, whispers weave,
Of magic born in hearts that believe.

In silver streams where starlight flows,
The mysteries of twilight grows.
Each flicker holds a tale untold,
In flickering glow, the night feels bold.

With every breath, the night aglow,
Where time bends lightly, soft and slow.
A dance of wonder, a dreamer's flight,
In realms alive with pure delight.

So close your eyes and drift away,
To glistening realms where shadows play.
In twilight's embrace, find peace, it seems,
Awakening softly, to twilight dreams.

# Gentle Breezes in the Shimmering Night

In a garden where the moonlight weaves,
Soft whispers dance among the leaves.
Stars twinkle like a hidden gem,
While dreams drift gently like a hymn.

The nightingale sings her sweet refrain,
Each note a drop of silvery rain.
Breezes weave through the fragrant blooms,
Awakening the slumbered rooms.

Fireflies flicker with a tender glow,
Guiding us where the soft winds blow.
A world wrapped in a velvet sigh,
Beneath the vast and starlit sky.

Crickets strum their soothing tune,
As shadows play beneath the moon.
In this haven, time stands still,
Our hearts entwined with quiet thrill.

With each breath, the magic grows,
In the stillness, the wonder flows.
Gentle breezes, a soft embrace,
In the shimmering night, we find our place.

# The Allure of Untraveled Whimsy

In a world where the wildflowers bloom,
Adventure lurks in every room.
Curious paths weave through the trees,
Whispers of secrets carried by the breeze.

Cobbled streets kissed by the dusk,
Every shadow holds a story to trust.
With laughter that twirls like leaves in flight,
The allure of whimsy ignites the night.

A lantern's glow calls us to roam,
Into the heart of the unknown tome.
Beneath the skies of a lavender hue,
Every moment feels fresh and new.

With every step on this unknown track,
The spark of dreams brings joy to unpack.
Following stars that twinkle and gleam,
We chase the echoes of a forgotten dream.

Here in the land of the untraveled, bold,
Stories await to be discovered and told.
With whimsy our guide, we'll forge our way,
Dancing through night till the dawn of day.

# Tapestries of Dreams in Twilight Mist

In twilight's mist, where wonders blend,
Each thread a tale that knows no end.
The sigh of evening weaves a spell,
A world where silent stories dwell.

Feathered whispers grace the air,
Unfolding mysteries hidden with care.
Colors swirl in a delicate stream,
As night wraps us in a tender dream.

Stars above like diamonds gleam,
In the fabric of a twilight dream.
Knitted hopes and gentle sighs,
Reflect the universe in our eyes.

The moon hangs low, a watchful guide,
A guardian of dreams that softly bide.
In this realm where hearts can soar,
Tapestries of dreams forever more.

As we wander through this perfect night,
We gather stars, our hearts alight.
In the twilight mist, we shall find,
Eternal wonders that bind the mind.

# Faery Secrets of the Overgrown Vale

In the vale where the wild roses grow,
Whispers of faeries soft and low.
Where shadows flicker and dance in light,
Their secrets hidden from mortal sight.

Mossy stones tell tales of yore,
The echo of laughter from a distant shore.
Glistening streams through the emerald glade,
Guard the dreams that the faeries have made.

Butterflies, jeweled in morning dew,
Flutter above where the magic is true.
In the flutter of wings, hope takes flight,
Guided by stars in the gentle night.

A tapestry weaved in nature's own hand,
Holds the allure of this enchanted land.
With every breath, the faery calls,
Echoing softly through the leafy halls.

In the overgrown vale of secrets old,
Whispers of dreams and stories untold.
Here in the heart of this magical space,
We find the faeries, their love, their grace.

## The Twinkle of Distant Starlight

In the velvet sky, the stars align,
Whispers of magic, through dusk they shine.
Dreamers gaze, with hearts so light,
Chasing the twinkle of distant starlight.

Galaxies dance in the shadowed night,
Casting their secrets in beams so bright.
Guiding lost souls on paths unknown,
Each flicker a tale, in the cosmos sown.

With every blink, a wish is born,
Hope and wonder, both gently worn.
In the silence, the universe sighs,
In the twinkle, our destiny lies.

Under the moon's watchful glow,
Fingers outstretched, as if to know.
The stories told in celestial lore,
Boundless adventures forever in store.

So let your dreams soar and take flight,
In the company of stars, all feels right.
For in their twinkle, we find our way,
A map of wonders, both night and day.

# Shadows Dancing with Ethereal Light

In enchanted woods where silence dwells,
Shadows embrace, weaving their spells.
Underneath trees, ancient and wise,
Dancing with light in a whimsical guise.

The moonbeams wink from branches above,
Illuminating secrets, like whispers of love.
With every flutter, the night comes alive,
Where dreams and shadows effortlessly thrive.

Footsteps echo in the soft, cool air,
Magic lingers, without a care.
Ethereal glow fuels the night's delight,
As shadows and spirits twirl in flight.

Hidden within the laughter of trees,
Are whispers of wishes carried by the breeze.
Mysteries cloaked in twilight's embrace,
As shadows and light intertwine in grace.

So let your heart wander, let your spirit free,
In the waltz of shadows, you'll find the key.
For ethereal light and the dance of night,
Reveal the magic hidden from sight.

# Mysteries Beneath the Flora's Glow

Beneath the foliage, where secrets seep,
Lies a realm where the ancients keep.
Petals unfurl, in colors so bright,
Revealing mysteries in the soft twilight.

Fungi and roots weave tales untold,
Guardians of lore, both timid and bold.
In their embrace, a magic weaves,
Whispering truths hidden under leaves.

A chorus of whispers fills the air,
With stories spun from the earth's own care.
Entities dwell in shadows below,
Where the wonders of flora endlessly grow.

Glimmers of life in each tiny vein,
Crimson and emerald, a vibrant chain.
Bugs and the blooms share a sweet refrain,
In nature's embrace, no soul feels pain.

So kneel by the earth, take a moment to see,
The wonders that dwell in each leaf and tree.
For the mysteries danced in the flora's glow,
Are tales of magic that gently flow.

# The Enigmas of Luminous Wanderers

Across the horizon, the wanderers glide,
With luminous hearts, in the night they confide.
Stars in their eyes, they traverse the skies,
Unveiling the enigmas where the cosmos lies.

With each gentle pulse, a story unfolds,
From galaxies swirling, with secrets untold.
They weave through the dark, like whispers of fate,
Luminous beings, we long to await.

A shimmer of hope in the black velvet sea,
Guiding our dreams, so wild and so free.
From the depths of the galaxy, they sing their tune,
The wanderers dance 'neath the watchful moon.

So when shadows gather and silence takes flight,
Listen for echoes of the wanderers' light.
For in every flicker, every shimmering beam,
Lies the promise of wonder, the birth of a dream.

Let their stories inspire, ignite your own spark,
Embrace the mysteries that dwell in the dark.
For the journey of life is both fragile and grand,
In the realms of the luminous, together we stand.

# Curiosities of the Ethereal Playground

In twilight's glow where shadows creep,
Whispers of magic softly seep.
Leaves shimmer with secrets untold,
In a realm where dreams unfold.

Dance of fireflies, waltzing near,
Each flicker sings of ancient cheer.
Mossy stones and laughter blend,
In this playground where wonders extend.

Beneath the boughs where night winds sigh,
Stars hang low, like dreams that fly.
Laughter echoes through the mist,
A moment's joy, a fleeting tryst.

Treading paths where few have trod,
Children of magic, the earth's own squad.
With every step, a new heartbeat,
In a realm where enchantments meet.

Joyful spirits chase the night,
In the dance of shadows, pure delight.
In this playground of the ethereal kind,
Curiosities of a spellbinding mind.

## Luminous Echoes of the Unexpected

In the silent forest, whispers stray,
Faint glimmers of the end of day.
They beckon from within the green,
Where unseen realms can be seen.

Moonbeams dance on leaves so bright,
Crafting tales of lost delight.
Echoes of laughter, light and free,
In the heart of twilight's mystery.

From hidden nooks, colors flare,
A painted canvas, beyond compare.
Each unexpected twist we find,
Leaves us humbled, heart entwined.

Glimmers of past, in shadows cast,
Memories linger, forever vast.
Each echo tells a secret story,
That wraps the night in timeless glory.

With every breath, we draw the night,
Luminous echoes, a gentle light.
In this dance of fate and lore,
We find the magic we search for.

### The Allure of the Hidden Barrow

Beneath the hill where shadows lie,
An ancient door hides, low and shy.
Covered in vines, in silence it waits,
A portal to worlds, behind heavy gates.

Whispers of tales, long forgotten,
Of treasures held, and battles fought in.
Each step toward the mound so grand,
Echoes of dreams that once spanned.

Starlit night, a daring quest,
To uncover what lies beneath the crest.
The allure of secrets buried deep,
Calls the brave, calls those who dare leap.

A silent oath to those who roam,
The barrow beckons as their home.
In those shadows, stories ignite,
A dance of memories, lost to night.

Thus, in twilight's soft embrace,
We yearn for the past, to trace.
The allure of the hidden barrow stands,
In the heart of the brave, in gentle hands.

# Tracings of the Sylvan Soul

In woodlands vast where spirits dwell,
Each rustling leaf tells a tale so swell.
The heart of nature beats so true,
Drawing the lost, the wanderers too.

Murmurs of trees sway soft and low,
In a dance of secrets only they know.
Each branch reaches, each root entwines,
In the embrace of soft moonshine.

From the brook's babble to the nightingale's song,
Echoes of life where we all belong.
The sylvan soul with joy abounds,
In the laughter of air, in the earth's sounds.

With every footfall upon the floor,
Nature opens wide its secret door.
Tracing paths that lead us near,
To a world alive, enchanting, clear.

In this haven, beneath the stars,
We find our dreams, our guiding czars.
The tracings of the sylvan soul,
Guide us back to where we are whole.

# Petals of the Hidden Forest

In the shade where shadows play,
Petals whisper to the day.
Mossy carpets, soft and green,
Secrets hide where none have seen.

Dewdrop jewels, glimmering bright,
Fluttering wings in soft twilight.
Gentle streams with crystal songs,
Nature's heart where all belongs.

Silver moonbeams, weaving light,
Stirring dreams in velvet night.
Ancient trees hold stories grand,
Guardians of this enchanted land.

Echoes rise and dance in air,
Whispers breathe of magic rare.
Fairy tales in every nook,
Written softly in a book.

Beyond the glade where wildwoods stand,
Adventures wait, forever planned.
Step by step, where wonders bloom,
Embrace the hidden forest's room.

# Where Time Winks and Wonders

In a world where moments twine,
Time stands still, a dance divine.
Every tick, a gentle chime,
Echoes weave in threads of rhyme.

Where age cannot wear its crown,
Youth's laughter slides the moments down.
Through horizons painted gold,
Whispers of the brave unfold.

Sunbeams catch the fleeting fair,
Dreams alight in open air.
Here, the past and future blend,
Each heartbeat a whispered friend.

Moments linger, softly spun,
Mosaic of the moon and sun.
Time's embrace, a gentle wave,
In this place, the heart is brave.

So let us stroll on paths untold,
Through the tales of young and old.
In this realm where wonders gleam,
Life's a never-ending dream.

# Paths of Gossamer and Stardust

In the twilight's tender glow,
Gossamer threads begin to flow.
Trails of starlight brush the air,
Guiding dreams to places rare.

With every step, a twinkling path,
Dancing shadows weave their math.
Gravity's pull, a gentle tease,
Whispers float upon the breeze.

Past the boundaries of the night,
Wonders rise beyond our sight.
Galaxies in the moon's embrace,
Infinite charm in every place.

Every star a tale untold,
In the heavens, we behold.
Through the cosmic dance, we stride,
On this journey, dreams abide.

Paths of light and threads of grace,
A symphony of time and space.
In this realm where wishes thrust,
Every heart finds hope and trust.

# The Veiled Journey of the Unseen

In shadows deep, where whispers dwell,
The unseen path begins to swell.
Cloaked in mystery, veiled in time,
Each step echoes a distant rhyme.

Through fog and mist, the heart does weave,
Beliefs and dreams we dare conceive.
Every heartbeat, a lantern's glow,
Guiding us where secrets flow.

Veils of night embrace the day,
Unfolding stories, come what may.
Magic dances softly near,
In the silence, truths appear.

Dream weavers spin their threads so fine,
In the weave, our fates entwine.
Steps uncharted, boldly tread,
On the road where souls are led.

Journey onward, hearts ablaze,
Through the mazes, dreams amaze.
The unseen draws us ever close,
In its arms, the spirit grows.

# Treasures Lost in the Whirl of Time

In shadows deep where whispers sigh,
The echoes of the past still fly,
Forgotten dreams on winds do roam,
With secrets held in time's own tome.

Each glimmer fades in twilight's grasp,
As memories within us clasp,
The ticking clock, a silent thief,
That robs us of our sweet belief.

Yet through the storm, hope dares to gleam,
A flicker caught in daylight's dream,
For treasures lost may still be found,
Amidst the whispers, all around.

So venture forth, brave hearts align,
In search of what is yours and mine,
For every shadow hides a light,
Within the depths of endless night.

## Alchemy of Glow and Glowworm

Beneath the boughs where twilight weaves,
The glowworms dance like dreams in leaves,
Their lanterns flicker, pure and bright,
In the embrace of velvet night.

With every spark, a story spins,
Of ancient woods and hidden sins,
The magic hums, a sweet refrain,
As secrets breathe through shadowed grain.

The alchemist of light so fair,
Turns darkness into golden air,
With each soft glow, a wish ignites,
Transforming whispers into flights.

So follow paths where starlight gleams,
And lose yourself in brightest dreams,
For in this dance of glow and shade,
The heart finds peace, the soul is made.

# Journey Through the Whispering Boughs

In forests thick where shadows play,
The whispering boughs guide the way,
With every turn, new tales unfold,
As ancient spirits weave their gold.

The rustling leaves, a gentle tune,
Underneath the watchful moon,
A pathway formed from light and sound,
Where wisdom waits, in lost and found.

Follow the breeze, let it entwine,
With echoes of a world divine,
For every step beneath the trees,
Invokes the past, the heart's sweet ease.

Journey forth, let magic flow,
In nature's arms where wonders grow,
For in these woods, so rich and vast,
The future dances with the past.

# The Allure of Celestial Misfits

Among the stars, where dreams take flight,
Lie misfits wrapped in endless night,
With tales of laughter, heartache, grace,
They wander through the vastest space.

From comets bright to moons obscure,
Their wanderlust is free and pure,
For every twinkle tells a story,
Of chaos woven into glory.

The universe, a jeweled thread,
Weaves destinies of those who tread,
In realms untouched by earthly bounds,
Their echoes dance in cosmic sounds.

So raise your eyes to skies so deep,
And listen close, for they shall speak,
In every heart beats their sweet song,
The misfits' love, where we belong.